# THE YEAR OF 2023

Another year, another war

Nohad T. Harati

*To my nephew, Philippe, who will reap
the rewards of a job well done.*

# INTRODUCTION

Although there were hopes that world inflation would fall in 2023, interest rates in the US were expected to reach the level of 5.00% and 5.25% in the middle of the year, remaining that high until the second half of 2024.

The European Central Bank (ECB), on its part, should have raised rates up to 4%, also maintaining them until the middle of 2024.

This level happened to be the double of what was the norm between 2005 and 2008, which could potentially increase the spreads of eurozone member states, as financial agents felt reluctant to purchase bonds of governments that were subsidizing the rising cost of energy.

As the war in Ukraine dragged on, expectations of oil reaching US$ 150 did not materialize as other commodity distribution channels allowed the product to flow to its destination. Similarly, other economic predictions, such as privately issued cryptocurrencies replacing the central role of the US dollar were dashed together with the collapse of FTX.

Both the pound and the euro had their "lost decade moment" as an endless Brexit process and Italy's "doom loop" responded to higher interest rates around the world, raised after the Fed.

Politically aligned countries wishing to guarantee better trade arrangements as well as some self-sufficiency struggled to find ways to emulate regional currencies similar to the euro, the enlarged BRICS being the obvious example, considering how different they were in terms of the free flow of capital and labor.

Securing supply chains and technology through industrial policy seemed to be a far more rational choice in face of external threats, even if that meant potentially higher inflation and a higher neutral rate, pushing forward the prospects of yet higher interest rates.

The benefits of artificial intelligence in terms of productivity or even China's ability to generate growth created more doubts than certainties, especially after war broke out in the Middle East.

# CHAPTER 1

## NEW PROTECTIONISM

Higher interest rates around the world would by themselves be enough to slow the global economy, given the impacts of restrictive credit. However, two other factors, not commonly commented on, but equally important, could define the intensity and duration of any fall.

The first is demographic: an increasing number of people living longer and having fewer children inevitably is captured in economic statistics. For example, in a period of just 20 years (1980-2000), GDP per capita in the world's major economies fell from 2.25% on average to something around 1.10%.

As the population ages, priorities change. As a result, investment in infrastructure, which takes a few years to bear fruits, is left out of the public budget in order to accommodate a growing retirement account.

**Non-replicable model**

There is not the slightest chance to replicate the growth pattern of the end of the last century, based on a young population that raised productivity levels in a macroeconomic environment that was quite receptive to reforms.

Nor will there be new gains coming from globalization, when taking into account the second factor for an economic slowdown: the protectionist shift by the US, whose measures partly came into effect in 2023.

With Washington's political elites seeking to also to reduce dependency on countries that would not necessarily play by their rules, the result is a major setback for international trade.

As other countries adjust to this reality, what is the best strategy?

**Subsidy costs**

A US$465 billion budget to boost the chip and renewable energy sectors showed the size of the American fire power.

The impacts of such big subsidies could be greater than initially foreseen, as they took the form of tax credits, which effectively depended on the quantity produced.

Nonetheless, assembling electronic components at Uncle Sam's was 55% more expensive than in Taiwan, keeping in mind that nowadays everything requires a chip in order to work. According to data gathered by the Boston Consulting Group (BCG), replicating the latest infrastructure in the sector would require anything between US$ 900 billion and US$ 1.2 trillion.

Not that it would guarantee leaps in innovation. The estimated values contemplated producing in the same way while guaranteeing self-sufficiency. Global chain values, in the end, would lose much of their operational efficiency as local content rules were implemented.

**Inefficiency**

More than finding an alternative place to China, which insisted on the zero covid strategy, the question was how other countries would respond to the rules imposed by the

Americans, which used them as an excuse to generating jobs and look after the environment, but were actually considered as being of national security.

Europe, already weakened by the energy shock that forced it to switch cheap Russian gas to LNG, was missing plenty of opportunities. For no other reason, the leaders of the European Union are pondering on how to adjust many of the rules designed for the proper functioning of the common European market.

## Supremacy

Behind the change in the direction of travel, two very clear purposes: to bring value chains closer to home, and to make the access to cutting-edge technologies more difficult.

Measures went beyond manufacturing facilities. For EV batteries, some countries had already banned mineral exports (such as Indonesia) or encouraged the development of new mines (such as Australia and Canada).

## Strategic investment

UNCTAD, the United Nations' agency responsible for collecting data on foreign investment in the world, calculated that more than half of projects suffered some form of restriction, largely due to the increased work scope of government agencies, notably in the US.

In these cases, how to anticipate problems?

This became a board room meeting question if laws became comprehensive enough to negatively impact the operations of publicly traded companies, all of which would observe in their share prices foreign authorities' discretion with regard to their investments.

## Export blockage

In addition to lower foreign direct investment (FDI), other measures included the suspension in the export of goods and services to certain countries, even when they were not subject to sanctions, such as Russia.

This made any update (software, components or expert advice) impossible, even on the occasions when there were no impediments whatsoever.

When it comes to international trade, game theory is always mentioned to illustrate its dynamics: when one participant (USA) breaks the rules, the others will do the same, as they try to minimize the damage from decisions not taken by consensus.

Consequently, the gains obtained in terms of scale and price are lost for good, as foreign direct investment reduces its participation from 5.3% of global GDP (data from 2007, the year before the financial crisis) to 2.3% of global GDP (most recent data, from 2021).

In this zero-sum game, where everyone offers more than the neighboring country, someone must lose so that the other can win.

Industrial policy and subsidies (60% of the total value sold, in the case of chips) can give a false sense that things are locally in check, even when they add little to future growth.

Whatever comparison is made with other moments of high interest rates, it is essential to take into account the influence of other elements. An aging population involves trade-offs with very practical implications: in the absence of growth, taxes necessarily have to increase in order to cover the bill, taking away resources that could be used for more productive purposes.

# CHAPTER 2

## SILICON VALLEY MINUS A BANK

Silicon Valley Bank (SVB), with assets of around US$200 billion, was closed on Friday, March 10th, following a string of negative news. Initially, a loss of US$ 1.8 billion. Soon after, a share offering to raise US$ 2.5 billion.

Its stock prices sank 60%, falling even further when it became clear that the chances of raising that amount of money were slim, as account holders rushed to transfer their funds. Until then, the bank prided itself of its expertise in providing financial services for startups.

It opened accounts and lent to those that were turned down by others, either because of their size or because of the poor quality of their guarantees.

**Venture capital boom**

Investments in venture capital (VC) reached US$ 638 billion between the years of 2012 and 2021, as new agents allocated resources in promising but risky companies.

Over time, specialized funds were joined by company's innovation arms as well as hedge and sovereign wealth funds looking for yields.

Despite being a niche market where only 10% of companies succeed, a world of low interest rates and highly priced assets justified the move. After all, historical data indicated that 70% of global companies started in the hands of vc funds.

The result could not be any different. As funds and startups received more resources from new investors, they deposited them in banks such as SVB, which then lent to others or, in their absence, invested in securities in order to make some money on spreads.

This seemed to work well until the outbreak of war in Ukraine.

**High inflation and high interest rates**

In the last quarter of 2022, the amount allocated to startups was already 67% lower when compared to the year before, occasion on which more than half of potential unicorns barely profited, largely due to its business model of free user access and high growth.

The macroeconomic environment was no longer favorable given the high level of interest rates, punishing a sector characterized by the culture of excess, useless diversification, in addition to the constant threat of crippling regulation and taxes.

The network effect, where the perceived value of a good or service grows with the number of users, had lost its magic. Higher prices and financing costs reduced people's purchasing power.

Consequently, the funding for new ideas dried up, in the same way that bonds, where banks invested the spare cash, reflected the higher cost of money.

Silicon Valley Bank found itself doubly exposed: startups, with less money coming in from investors, began to withdraw from their accounts. In order to honor these withdrawals, SVB liquidated its bond portfolio, receiving much less than what it paid for.

## Out with the tourists

With the fall of the Nasdaq index, companies that not even were part of it suffered. Many strategies no longer make sense, such as forming diversified portfolios of startups.

Founders also were no longer interested in selling their businesses to buy pieces of others. As new rounds of investment became necessary, they were inevitably diluted in their holdings.

Over time, the venture capital industry shifted from doing the fieldwork to just making the money. Funds that were invested in startups for years began to circulate more freely between them, turning vc into credit malls or asset management companies.

Transactions between competing funds occurred for other reasons, as new assets and players (a consequence of several years of low interest rates) were added to that ecosystem.

## Bank run

SVB's problems were aggravated by Silicon Valley's own insiders.

Unlike a common bank run, where average people fear for their life savings deposited in a bank under momentary difficulties, the venture capital managers themselves advised startups to withdraw their money.

Some estimates indicated that 93% of deposits were not insured, given the large base of business accounts.

Another concern was the possibility of other financial institutions in similar conditions, with their undervalued portfolios potentially spreading the damage. More banks would then be forced to liquidate positions at a loss in order to honor new withdrawals, something that the Fed intended to avoid by providing emergency credit lines.

As the years went by, it became clear that opportunities were dwindling. Meanwhile, IPOs, for reflecting rocky market conditions, were no longer suitable as "exit strategies".

As an example, still in 2022, a hedge fund had somewhere around 70% to 80% of its portfolio in cash, showing the enormous difficulty in making the right kind of bets. Volatility did not help even mature candidates, qualified for listing on stock exchanges.

Many were turning to other, most obvious options: artificial intelligence companies with practical solutions, "climate friendly" technologies, and highly complex manufacturing, due to protectionism and the resurgence of industrial policy.

Given the size of many sovereign wealth funds, managed with national interests in mind, the distance between startup and investor may have shrunk to a hallway, far from Silicon Valley.

# CHAPTER 3

## MEET THE INTEREST RATE RISK

Fifteen years after the 2008 financial crisis, was the world doomed to yet more problems within the banking system?

Observing the news in mid-March, it was difficult not to remember the "Occupy Wall Street" movement, the rise of gold and the anarchic groups claiming the need for a currency that was not controlled by "reckless" governments and central banks.

At that time, the focus was on institutions considered too big to fail that took advantage of the real estate bubble by giving credit to people with poor scores (ironically, nothing very different from the leverage FTX fomented before going bust).

As in any crisis, along with the government intervention, stricter rules which, for the case of banks, was the following: to get rid of low-quality loans and keep safer US Treasury bonds instead.

### Too small to bother

Even though part of the regulation applicable to large banking institutions was reversed through lobbying during Donald Trump's term, at no time were other agents obliged to mark to market bond portfolios held to maturity.

This explained the difficulties of Silicon Valley Bank (SVB).

While the world of low interest rates did not make the shortest securities profitable, the bank purchased longer-term securities in in order to obtain higher returns.

With the onset of interest rate hikes (and the reversal of this process), US$ 620 billion in bonds became worthless, even though losses were only accounted for as they were sold to honor depositor withdrawals.

To understand what that meant for the banking system, a 10% drop in bond value would be enough to eliminate at least 25% of a banks' equity, causing more shares to be issued in order to plug the hole.

**Mirrored balance sheet**

Considering that SVB's "app bank run" started with people familiar with its modus operandi, what else did they find?

Roughly speaking, a bank's balance sheet is the inverse of a company's balance sheet. On the asset side (left side), operations with third parties and, on the liability side (right side), depositor funds.

At the beginning of 2022 (hence, before the rate hike), U.S. bank assets, amounting to approximately $24 trillion, were distributed, by order of liquidity, as follows:

- Just over 14% in cash
- A quarter in government bonds and mortgages
- Almost half in loans

Liabilities amounted to US$19 trillion in deposits, half of which were covered by the Federal Deposit Insurance Corporation (FDIC).

At first glance, good numbers. However, if half of uninsured account holders withdrew their money, 190 US banks would not have an extra US$1 to honor any additional withdrawals.

First, because bonds with longer maturities are less liquid

(harder to sell without a discount on its fair price). Second, because the remaining resources are invested in the real economy and, therefore, cannot be demanded promptly.

## Interest rate risk

In the post-crisis years, US Treasuries were believed to be safer than loans, although both carried the interest rate risk if and when inflation became an issue.

For no other reason, the decision of the Federal Reserve (Fed) to create a special one-year credit line, accepting as collateral securities at their face value (as opposed to their market value).

In practice, any bank would hand over its portfolio in exchange for the immediate access to funding, reducing any worries about unaccounted for losses.

## Lender of all resorts

Between 1863 and 1913, the US faced 8 banking crises, with serious economic consequences, which led to the creation of the Federal Reserve System and its regional representatives.

Shortly thereafter, the regulation for deposit insurance. However, to prevent banks from taking too many risks, authorities set a limit on the interest rates they could offer depositors.

Things worked well until the 1970s, when the first oil shock, stemming from an Organization of Petroleum Exporting Countries (OPEC) boycott, caused inflation to explode and economic growth to slow sharply.

The Fed took on a broader role, liquidating failed banks, insuring deposits outside the FDIC, injecting liquidity into the banking system, and even bailing out a hedge fund (Long-Term Capital Management).

Despite the different strategies, they all had the same

purpose: to stop the panic and avoid contagion, even if some financial agents had to be "sacrificed" along the way.

Along the decades, they acquired experience to also address other issues, such as the economic response to covid-19, based on ample liquidity and the acceptance of a greater variety of securities as collateral.

Truth be told, no banking institution survives if all account holders withdraw at the same time.

That was exactly what Ben Bernanke, Douglas Diamond and Philip Dybvig, winners of the 2022 Nobel Prize in Economics argued through their extensive research, many of which used to impose minimum banking standards.

Although fixed-income securities are quickly repriced downwards as interest rates reach higher levels, they are not the only assets the banking system holds, remembering tighter financial conditions also impact loans negatively, given the increase in defaults.

Nonetheless, it was feared such a generous Fed would again encourage moral hazard.  After all, US banks would pay 4.5% for the privilege, but if the return on their assets was lower than that, they would report losses each quarter.

Fortunately, some lessons were learned: 2008 style bail-outs were definitely out of question, given the levels of public debt. Furthermore, it is now widely known that overly strict regulations favor the dark side of finance (aka "shadow banking").

The big question mark was more related not exactly to the next domino to fall but rather the next distortions that could be uncovered ahead.

# CHAPTER 4

## THE FED'S TOOLBOX

Even with a handful of banks facing crisis, several central banks raised their interest rates.

After all, the mission to fight inflation prevailed, as some factors were taken into account by monetary authorities. The first concerned the propensity of governments to spend more.

With what exactly? The extensive list included more pensions, the infrastructure needed for the energy transition, not to mention the return of industrial policy, as countries sought self-sufficiency and regional trading arrangements.

Another issue was inflationary dynamics itself. Taking into account other oil shocks of geopolitical origin, similar to the one resulting from the invasion of Ukraine, it is clear that prices take time to go the desired way.

**The process of raising rates**

When a central bank decides to raise interest rates, it starts a process that affects the entire economy, slowing it down.

In the same way that people have accounts with banks, banks have their accounts with the central bank, where they deposit their funds. They can either be borrowed by third parties or remain there, earning interest.

It is a system that, just like a in a building, few pay attention to. Daily, money and bonds (which serve as collateral) change hands without much difficulty.

The problem arises when the perception of risk changes among agents. While assets remain as safe as they ever were, the same cannot be said about the lending they foster. Often, it is not even necessary for a default to take place, just an increase in the probability of that happening.

That said, big changes in interest rates modify the natural order of things. In the case of the Silicon Valley Bank, the securities held served perfectly as guarantees to honor ordinary withdrawals.

**Redoing the math**

Roughly speaking, the rate set by the central bank determines all others, which means that banks redo the math to calibrate their credit lines. This increase is reflected in the value of loan installments, leaving less for consumption.

The effects become visible to everyone. With people spending less, companies also invest less, reducing economic activity.

Political pressure comes from the simple fact that there is no way to control high inflation without imposing some kind of sacrifice, which essentially depends on the credibility of the monetary authority (if the central bank gives in to pressure, the share of sacrifice is bigger).

Taking into account the time needed between the action (increase in interest rates) and the response (consistent reduction in inflation), the less "noise" observed in this period, the smaller the negative impacts on consumption, employment, and asset values.

**The Fed's toolbox**

Ben Bernanke was once asked whether interest rate hikes were adequate to deflate speculative asset bubbles before they did more damage to the economy.

His answer was that the Federal Reserve (Fed) had a "toolbox": while macro-prudential regulation guided market participants, interest rates controlled inflation.

The curious thing was that, more recently, it was quite common to hear the opposite question: Shouldn't the Fed reduce interest rates to ease the pain of the loss in value in banks' portfolios?

Jerome Powell, like Bernanke, chose the politically correct answer: "isolated problems within the banking system, if not resolved, undermine confidence in others". Then he added: "Without price stability, the economy doesn't work for everyone."

In the US, February data had shown inflation of 6%, that is, triple the country's target. Furthermore, with yet another emergency line, the Fed demonstrated that its "toolbox" had been upgraded.

Unlike the 2008 crisis and the beginning of the pandemic, the Fed seemed more restrained in its response, perhaps with the aim of avoiding further problems.

**Monetary confusion**

At the beginning of 2022, the Fed implemented quantitative tightening (the reverse process of quantitative easing or "QE"), a mechanism by which it "created" money to buy government bonds of various maturities.

Month by month, a certain amount of bonds matured, which caused them to drop off the Fed's balance sheet, reducing liquidity within the system. Between 2022 and early 2023, $600 billion was eliminated that way.

The value returned to US$ 300 billion, as emergency lines

were offered to stop the panic surrounding the Silicon Valley Bank.

Despite different objectives (quantitative tightening as a change in the Fed's balance sheet and emergency lines as something more specific), there may be doubts about the Fed's real intentions in future crises.

One of the great advantages of QE resided in the fact that it was much cheaper for the government to finance itself by paying interest on reserves than by bond auctions, where transactions are made at higher and more volatile market rates.

In theory, more restrictive financial conditions, caused by problems within the banking system, would already be enough to stop the Fed, due to a natural reaction to the increase of risk.

This is perhaps even more true for Europe, where the banking sector has a greater weight.

Looking back, the Fed has learned a lot about how to stimulate the economy when interest rates are already very low, which is no longer the current reality.

Given the challenges posed (supply shocks, changes in global value chains and climate change), monetary authorities are still betting on their credibility. Without it, there is no tool that works.

# CHAPTER 5


## FRAGMENTATION


Considering the geopolitical shift since the war in Ukraine began, were there any real risks for the US dollar? Would BRICS countries themselves launch a new currency of their own? Under such uncertain times, economic predictions are as good as anybody's guess.

Nonetheless, a few elements had to be taken into account.

**US supremacy**

The US still led in terms of wealth, productivity and innovation, as it was responsible for 25% of all that is produced in the world, even when considering the growing importance of China in international trade.

Additionally, it had a 58% share of the G7's GDP. Unlike the other members of the group, it benefited from populational growth, which turned into greater productivity.

Innovation, on its part, was up to companies, which spent a lot on research and development, given the size of the US consumer market (which allowed them to dilute costs) and the US financial markets, where investments were channeled.

For all these reasons, it was very unlikely for the dollar to lose its relevance.

**The rest of the world**

At least 4 billion people, or something like more than half of the world's population, lived in countries that preferred not to take sides in sovereign disputes.

Among them, absolutely no ambition to form large economic blocks, considering the complexity faced by the European Union (countries with different realities, but that followed the same rules).

## Non-alignment

In the 1950s, a group of countries banded together to counterweight a world then divided between the US and the Soviet Union, without much success.

Failure was due to a list of characteristics they did not share: a common view, a permanent seat in the United Nations' security council, economic and military weight and, last but not least, dynamic technology and finance sectors.

By the end of the Cold War, it had already been forgotten.

If the same countries were to unite again, they would face similar challenges, as they depend on certain imports (technology and weapons). The difference in relation to the past is that they became more representative (approximately 18% of global GDP, higher than the European Union).

## Open for business

Concerned with their own development, they had a very pragmatic view, negotiating with anyone, while trying to attract new businesses. Among the goods traded among them, 43% were of North American and European origin, 19% Chinese and Russian, and 30% from the rest of the world.

Given this standard, it was expected that US and European banks, tasked with enforcing sanctions, remained relevant for processing international payments, whether in the current system or in any future system with digital currencies issued by central banks.

## Alone or as a group

In this new scenario, each one outlined their own strategy, sometimes acting alone, sometimes together.

The Organization of the Petroleum Exporting Countries (OPEC) cut production by 4% just as China became Saudi Arabia's biggest trading partner, replacing the US.

The BRICS, made up of Brazil, Russia, India, China and South Africa, on their part, were evaluating at the same time whether to let Saudi Arabia and Iran in, also capitalizing their bank.

Among them, no one denied a certain skepticism with the world order. As much as the World Bank could be led by an Indian, it was highly unlikely that the International Monetary Fund (IMF), always led by a European, would be presided by a South African or a Brazilian.

## When money is not the only factor

In any case, implementing a common currency, as had been suggested, needed to take into account any previous work, such as linking all the involved currencies to a main one.

As long as China remained reluctant to abandon its capital controls, none of it would happen, especially as any fixed exchange rate mechanism hardly has any use when volatility strikes.

## The role of the IMF

Created in 1944, its function was to promote trade and manage the exchange rate system established at the time ("Bretton Woods"). With the breakdown of this arrangement decades later, the IMF began lending to countries facing difficulties.

Throughout the 1980s, with the Latin American debt crisis and, with the financial crisis in Asia that followed, the fund carried out several rescue operations, under very strict conditions, which did not necessarily bring the expected results.

Nowadays, 30% of the borrowed resources are in the hands of Argentina, with 21 being the most recent number of countries waiting in line for help, either because of the pandemic or because of the increase in the costs of imported fuel and food (a consequence of the war in Ukraine).

Whatever dynamics the world economy adopts, new issues will have to be addressed such as security, foreign debt, and climate change, all of which involve China, the main business partner to 120 countries and, for many of them, the lender of first and last resort.

In the rest of the world, countries that act alone or together. For anyone wanting to imagine what the future could be like, the answer might as well be here.

# CHAPTER 6

## REGULATION AND THE CRYPTO WORLD

Did difficulties faced by banking institutions justify the search for other types of investments? In the world of finance, extreme attitudes only lead to disastrous results, which shows, above all, the virtues of a diversified portfolio.

Feuds between the traditional and the crypto market aside, it is worth highlighting how financial markets use innovations to their best interests, even before many sectors do the same.

**Early adopters**

Broadly speaking, regulated institutions bypass cryptocurrencies basically due to the lack of a more consistent legal framework, not to mention the enormous volatility.

But this does not mean that they do not study their technology ("tokenization") very carefully when aiming to reduce costs and improve processes, which even allows for other business opportunities.

In the meantime, they adopt a cautious stance, opting for products that lack technical specifications that are too hard to swallow (such as ETFs), capturing a good part of the investors who already use these instruments.

However, financial innovation cannot limit itself to index funds.

## The USA and its regulatory chaos

In the US, the convergence of many bills waiting for approval and barely any consensus. Just as a series of laws were imposed after the 2008 crisis, something similar was expected after FTX went bust.

The way crypto companies were audited only added to the sense of chaos: the Securities and Exchange Commission (SEC), responsible for securities, shared regulatory duties with the Commodity Futures Trading Commission (CFTC), in charge of activities involving commodities. Among them, the numerous state agencies.

All tightening the siege simultaneously.

## Playing the sheriff

In common, a desire to uncover financial frauds or impose rules by other means.

For the authorities, exchange crashes at the end of 2022 served as very convenient examples to "reinforce" the need to defend small investors, unaware of the risks they are exposed to.

As for companies that claimed to be outside US jurisdiction and, hence, not subject to its laws, the message was quite clear: they were unable to do business with US companies.

Impacted by somewhat arbitrary measures, some local players decided to cross the Atlantic.

## The legislation of the European Union

The European Union (EU) approved the regulation applicable to Cryptoassets Markets (MiCA), expected to be implemented in July, after ratification by the 27 member states.

One of the advantages of this set of laws is that it would be adopted in stages, giving time for participants to adapt. Another positive point was that it was widely discussed, unlike the fierce enforcement chosen by US authorities.

## MICA 2.0

However, it can be said that the time of the regulator is not the same as that of the business world, which meant that laws that would be put into effect already needed updates, such as the actions to be taken when an important exchange defaults (in a mechanism similar to that designed for banks after the 2008 crisis).

Still, there was some merit to the initiative. First, as with other financial products, it was enough to register in one EU country in order to operate freely inside the economic bloc.

Additionally, there was a clearer definition of the roles of the banking authority and the agency responsible for securities, avoiding many of the problems seen in the US.

## Illegal leverage

Despite the efforts to select the assets that would back stablecoins, European law remained quite conservative, leaving out decentralized finance (DeFi), loans involving cryptoassets, and non-fungible tokens (NFTs).

The approach was in line with the development of the digital euro (digital currency under development by the European Central Bank), where there was even greater concern in identifying operations, putting an end to crypto anonymity.

The failure of Silicon Valley Bank and the venture capital industry, as explained in chapter 2, did not stop other interested parties from acting. In the first quarter of 2023, mergers and acquisitions (M&A) between digital asset companies reached record levels.

They planned to gain ground not by launching new cryptocurrencies or promoting speculation, but rather by developing the necessary digital infrastructure, which could eventually be shared by a wider group of countries, as it happens in the international financial system.

## CBDC standards

Despite high interest rates, everyone with a stake in the game was looking for ways to prepare for when the opposite happened, given the predictable movement towards investments with higher returns.

Hence, the challenge remained in understanding the technological aspects so that updating current rules, exhaustively tested in crises, did not jeopardize the potential gains offered by innovation.

Central bank digital currencies (CBDCs) would set the environment for crypto payments and the trading of cryptoassets.

This is how other attributes, such as their use for monetary policy (negative interest rates, as implemented in Europe in the past), or for other purposes, such as stimulating the economy or certain sectors (with the so-called "programmable money") will create a minimum standard.

Whether financial institutions will continue with their due roles or whether transactions will be exclusively "retail" (as with personal digital wallets in China) is a decision that ultimately lies with the preferences and fears of each society.

# CHAPTER 7

## CHATGPT

Artificial intelligence (AI) seemed to be something limited to tech labs until the emergence of ChatGPT. Controversial knowledge tool, it generates both admiration for the possibilities it offers and concern due to inconsistencies in the answers it provides.

Advancing at an astonishing speed, it is a fact that this revolutionary technology will be among us, performing some quite ordinary tasks, which brings up the big question: what is its impact on the economy?

**Forecasts**

As with anything related to the world of startups and technology, predictions were as optimistic as ever.

Still, part of the financial market showed skepticism, when taking into account the role of high interest rates in the world, which reduced the future cashflows of publicly traded companies while raising their financing costs at the same time.

Looking back, it's easy to point to the many benefits of innovation. However, it is always accompanied by other factors, which prevents it from being measured individually.

Robert Fogel, winner of a Nobel Prize in Economics,

illustrated this in his study of US railroads, responsible for leaving an essentially agricultural America behind. His conclusion was that the impact of the railway system itself was small, bringing to light other, equally important issues.

## Economic impacts

First, it's not hard to imagine a Google or Meta of artificial intelligence (in this case, OpenAI), given that companies that develop disruptive technologies take a good share of the market and the profits.

Typically, this is due to barriers to entry or a lack of options. For example, GPT-4 was "trained" at a cost of $100 million, with an in-house technology. Nonetheless, it is likely other companies will emerge as competitors, given the amount of information shared online.

In addition to them, it would make perfect sense to include others that already exist and that might participate in the same ecosystem. That would be the case of Nvidia, famous for its gaming boards, but which also has data centers to help chatbots "learn to think".

In terms of jobs, OpenAI itself calculates that something like 80% of the US labor market would have at least 10% of its activities changed. Impacts would be profound.

## AI or a whole team?

In a notorious New York Times article, it reported the case of a lawyer who used an artificial intelligence tool to study a legal proceeding that had more than 400 pages.

After a few minutes and, fortunately for him, the result was a summary that included information of an important topic that had been left out, but that was fundamental to nail a favorable outcome.

Would AI be the jobs serial killer? By and large, many economists have already been caught off guard when it comes to the labor market. In 2013, a study by the University of Oxford had predicted that automation would eliminate nearly half of jobs in the U.S. in a period of just 10 years.

Excluding the most recent developments, such as the return of industrial policy, what was observed was exactly the opposite. In countries like Japan, Singapore and South Korea, where robotics predominates, the unemployment rate is quite low.

The same can be said about the U.S. Jobs defined as "at risk of being wiped out for technological reasons" showed no significant downward trend, according to the Bureau of Labor Statistics.

**Regulation**

As much as the announcement that IBM would stop hiring workers for certain functions may be intimidating, there will always be sectors where AI can't handle everything, as it the case of healthcare and education, just to name a few.

Hence, as noted on several occasions in the past, the process of eliminating jobs is slower than initially anticipated, given regulation and the weight of public policies.

Also, it can be said that every technology has its limitations, mainly due to human nature. The smartphone used for work is the same one used for fun.

Given this unavoidable truth, what is the role of governments with regards to artificial intelligence? It is a fact that several growth engines (renewable energy, chip manufacturing, biotechnology) depend on this type of tool. What will be their priorities, given the need to bring together all parties such as research, infrastructure, human capital, financial markets, etc.?    In the race for self-sufficiency, much of the technological capability required is not even available to countries outside the G7.

With so many possibilities, the worst scenario would be for authorities to shun AI, with the excuse that it only serves to cause chaos, such as the presence of very powerful companies (Big Techs) in societies without work.

Perhaps the most important thing is to stimulate people to think for themselves as well as learn, not delegating the decision-making process whatsoever.  Without the proper skills, innovation, with all its intelligence, will not bring any progress.

# CHAPTER 8

## PEAK CHINA

At the beginning of 2021, China was all over the news, with its economy growing an average of 9% per year since the late 70s.

Estimates from the International Monetary Fund at the time pointed to Xi Jinping's land as the largest economy as early as 2030, largely due to the region concentrating more people than all the rest of the world combined.

**Growth at any cost**

The previous year, in the middle of the pandemic, the Chinese economy had grown by 2.3%, thanks to its centralized and planned way of functioning.

Even when things didn't go so well, opportunities abroad compensated for the downturn, which explained the large amount of funding for infrastructure projects around the world.

More than a showcase to expose its giant industrial capacity and obtain concessions, it was a way to put its young and highly qualified workforce (engineers) to work.

In order to do so, they relied on the latest technologies, considering the large number of startups in the country, fostered by the breakneck pace of Chinese entrepreneurship.

## Deceleration

After 1016 days closed to the outside world, China was expected to yet again do what it had done for a long time: boost the world economy.

But some evidence showed that this might no longer be possible. "Peak China" was nothing more than the beginning of its economic deceleration. In this scenario, it would no longer overtake the US, acting rather as a matching superpower.

This change in perspective was no accident. At the beginning of the year, the United Nations (UN) already predicted that India's population would surpass that of China by 2023. As in other parts of the world, the Chinese population was also aging, with few couples having children.

Compared to the US, the country has 4.5 times more people of working age, a number that would fall to 3.4 times by 2050, reaching 1.7 times before 2100. That said, the number of Chinese people of working age could fall another 25% in just a generation (25 years).

To address such a decline, increased productivity could be part of the answer for growth, were it not for the use of a larger share of resources to care for the elderly.

## Outdated model

The marginal benefit of any large-scale construction, be it a new road or a new housing development, had run into its limits.

The development model based on the sale of land by local governments for construction shifted the problem to companies, which became also responsible for meeting the growth targets demanded by the Chinese political elite.

Other sectors were nowhere near investing more in the country as the experience with the draconian way in which authorities prevented the spread of the covid-19 virus left an unpleasant mark among the business community.

Executives were not only reluctant to modernize their manufacturing parks, but also assessed the impacts of industrial policy in their countries of origin.

**New global priorities**

With the fall of the Soviet Union in the 1990s, a new economic order, based on little government interference and globalization, greatly benefited China. If before there was an economic logic where everyone shared the gains, the truth is that priorities had changed.

National security issues (a result of the war in Ukraine) and climate change (perceived at various events over the past year) had moved up in the agenda, as it had put growth at any cost aside.

On the first topic, the application of sanctions was quite illustrative. When Russia invaded Ukraine, the 27 member states of the European Union (EU) discussed at length whether to boycott Russian gas as a form of retaliation.

The fear, exposed mainly by economic agents, was that such a measure would be a fatal blow to Europe. In the end, the mild weather helped, but many economists argued that everyone would adapt to new conditions, which would do less damage than expected.

Security issues would also hold back China's growth as restrictions applied to certain technologies. This would be observed in the "reshoring" process, where value chains are brought closer to home, especially if their production is deemed strategic.

As a result, foreign direct investment would lose an even

bigger share in global GDP.

Climate change, however, would represent the biggest restriction of all. If weather events cross borders and can even occur simultaneously, a minimum of cooperation would be desirable.

Nonetheless, each country implements its "eco-friendly" program without considering its effect on the aggregate, generating a waste of considerable resources given public spending limitations.

## The impossible task of making predictions

Demographic changes and productivity levels generate different outcomes over time, not to mention the impacts of exchange rates on how each country interacts with the rest of the world.

To identify which one is likely to lead, it's important to bear in mind the 3 attributes of any superpower: economic efficiency, as well as military and economic might.

Measuring them is relatively easy: productivity represents the first, the military budget, in relation to the broader economy points to the second, while the rest of GDP, in comparison to global GDP, gives the magnitude of the third.

In order to threaten the global order, the potential candidate must excel in all of them.

# CHAPTER 9

## WHAT ABOVE 2% MEANS

For economists, the future will feature more inflation and less growth, based on the analysis of the years 2021 and especially 2022. In the U.S. and Europe, core inflation, which disregards volatile items such as fuel and food, exceeded 5% (well above the 2% target).

There was a certain optimism in the financial markets, for absolute lack of bad news.

After all, oil prices were quite well behaved when compared to a year ago, even with the Organization of the Petroleum Exporting Countries (OPEC) cutting production. The same lull was observed in China, which performed worse than expected.

There was a lack of global dynamism, which could hurt economic growth, especially after a few mid-sized U.S. banks fell on their knees.

**Higher inflation target**

But unlike other occasions in the past, public budgets were nowhere near aligned with the objective of fighting inflation.

As much as central banks are independent, what would happen if they took a more flexible stance towards their inflation targets, thus avoiding freezing economic activity?

Some big shots on Wall Street believed in the hypothesis. Not that inflation would overshoot, but rather contemplating a target higher than 2%, which then could turn into 3% or more.

Weakness on the part of central banks? No, just the reckoning that other forces were at work in the economy, which would require a much greater sacrifice to return to the original goal.

**More than just a number**

The higher inflation gets, the more unstable it becomes.

Using historical data from the U.S. economy as an example, in the years when the consumer index rose by as much as 5%, average inflation for the next 12 months hovered around 1.8%.

For instance, after a 2% inflation, chances were it would remain between 0.2% and 3.8% (almost double the target).

Using some calculations made by The Economist, with inflation at 4%, a person who purchased a 10-year U.S. bond would receive only 68% of the original amount at maturity.

Following the same logic, the longer the term of the bond, the greater the impact of higher inflation. In the case of a 30-year bond, considering the same 4% inflation, the percentage of the original value returned at maturity would fall to 31%.

Would it be the case to buy inflation-linked bonds? Not necessarily, because only 8% of the US public debt is made up of this type of option.

**The challenge of investing**

Imagine that a large group of investors left the stock market, quite popular, and went to another that is a favorite in the scenario of low growth and high inflation:

the commodity market.

This group would have two options: trade in the physical market, with all the costs associated with transporting and properly storing the commodity, or in the much smaller futures market (equivalent to 1% of the size of the U.S. stock market), inevitably fueling another financial bubble.

Not even the most traditional investment alternative would escape. Using Turkey as an example, in just two years, the positive change in the value of real estate in Istanbul exceeded 480%.

Even when taking into account the effects of the currency devaluation, the increase was greater than in any other economy in the world, according to a study by the Bank for International Settlements (BIS).

As a consequence of high prices, rents were above the country's average income, even after successive increases in the minimum wage. Although there was a shift in monetary policy after the elections, with a 6.5% interest rate increase, prices continued to rise.

With the "dollar inflation," it would not be hard to imagine the same happening in more desirable cities around the world.

**Inflation at the center of everything**

With governments prone to spending more and a world economy struggling to get off the ground, perhaps the time had come to accept that inflation will be the determinant factor in financial decisions.

Under these circumstances, all asset classes are repriced, taking into account their attractiveness in the face of an inflationary environment. Investment portfolios are altered not only by this characteristic, but also by the additional degree of uncertainty.

After all, given a modest economic growth, there is only so much one can do in terms of raising taxes or cutting public spending. Consequently, inflation may be precisely the most efficient way to reduce the real value of any debt, a reality that has accompanied emerging economies for a long time.

For them, the investment in dollars represented the only safe haven when everything else could potentially go wrong. Looking forward, this same investment could lose 30% of its purchasing power in a period of only 10 years in case U.S. inflation doubled.

# CHAPTER 10

## DIGITAL PAYMENTS

As much as financial transactions by internet are related to fintechs, other agents, such as governments and banks, have also favored the use of technology.

Globally speaking, this allowed the development of 3 different models:

- Digital checking accounts and bank cards (prevalent in rich countries);
- "Super apps" with payment functions, offered by large technology companies (common in China);
- Payment systems to replace the use of cash (chosen by emerging countries such as India, with UPI, and Brazil, via Pix).

The analysis of the last model perhaps is the worthiest, for its simplicity and the remarkable results achieved, especially when taking into account that this group ("emerging economies") contains countries that have derailed (Argentina and Turkey) and where the volatility of cryptocurrencies is the only refuge for instability and hyperinflation.

**M-PESA**

M-PESA, created in 2007 in Kenya, served as the initial inspiration. It was intended to allow users to send money via SMS messages, given the low number of people with bank accounts in the country.

Observing their evolution, it can be said that these systems are designed with some principles in mind. First, they are stimulated by the government and do not have the purpose of profit.

Another feature is that they are open, that is, other participants can join, fostering competition.

A third peculiarity is that they are used anywhere (a QR Code and a mobile phone with a camera is all that is needed for the payment to be made quickly).

**FedNow**

With so much going on, one might wonder why the US still used an old and slow system to settle payments. Unlike in many parts of the world, Americans used different payment methods for different purposes, be it the payment of a utility bill or an online purchase.

Besides, financial institutions profited by investing the proceeds while transactions were not cleared, which explained why some decided not to join FedNow in the first place.

**Regulation**

One of the main complaints is that these systems are incomplete as they lack some form of insurance for operational failures, even when taking into account the rise of central bank digital currencies (CBDCs).

Until big techs announced their intention to create their own currencies, no government had felt threatened by the idea of losing control over its own financial system.

Since then, roughly 114 countries were addressing the issue. In common, the establishment of some rules, such as a limit per account and the absence of any interest payment, keeping banks in the game.

However, in places where the payment system is efficient and comprehensive, no additional advantage was observed when adopting sovereign digital currencies, other than the possibility to collect data from the economy or use "programmable money", which imposed the conditions under which it could be spent.

**Multitude of objectives**

It is undeniable that any country had all the interest in the world in digital payment systems for somewhat obvious reasons: they facilitate the collection of taxes.

Another rather laudable goal would be financial stability. If the transfer of a large amount of money is motivated by rumors on social media (as the most recent banking crisis has shown), it is expected that some rules would avoid this type of risk.

After all, an economy only develops when there is a wider range of financial services, including insurance and loans, only available due to the data collected by digital means.

Like any new technology, everyone had a lot to gain in terms of agility and efficiency, but in order for money to move easily around the world and generate the much-desired growth, countries had to develop a common standard so that these systems could operate between themselves, not least to break free from the infrastructure built around the US dollar.

# CHAPTER 11

## DEFLATION IN AN INFLATIONARY WORLD

At the beginning of August, some not very encouraging news from China: a 14% drop in exports, one more construction company struggling to honor its financial commitments, in addition to a negative value in the annual price index.

Coming out of the pandemic much later than the rest of the world, the country was expected to quickly recover the lost ground, repeating something similar to the spectacular performance of the early 2000s, raising concerns that this would generate new inflationary pressures, demanding even higher interest rates.

While the US and the European Union observed annual inflation rates of 3% and 6.4% respectively, China registered a deflation of 0.3%. This would not be unprecedented were it not for the same trend observed in wholesale prices for 10 consecutive months.

Chinese products sold abroad were cheaper, while investments out of China and measures taken against technology companies in the past meant that approximately one in five young people could not find work.

**Deflation**

The Chinese economy has not escaped volatility in food prices, something that would inevitably show in the indices. However, the surprise was due to the service sector, which did not take off, even with the opening of the economy.

The real estate market also failed to react, undermining expectations of increases in sales not only of residential units, but also of home related products. In the main Chinese cities, sales were 28% lower when compared to the same month in 2022.

Being a centralized economy, more was expected from local authorities as numbers were made public.

Announcements were limited to reducing barriers to entry and granting intellectual property rights to companies wishing to invest. Additionally, measures included stimulating consumption and tourism, as well as a certain flexibility for workers from rural areas to move to cities.

Unlike other occasions, help will not come from the outside world either.

With interest rates high elsewhere, demand for Chinese exports suffered. As a consequence, companies were rapidly reducing their inventories and, unless there was a reversal in this scenario, dismissing their employees, with significant impacts on the consumption of goods and services.

## China plus one

Tariffs on international trade, initially imposed by the Trump administration, showed their cumulative effects. After two decades, it was the first time that the US traded more with Mexico and Canada than with China.

However, statistics did hide a curious fact: countries that received investments previously directed to China (India,

Mexico, and Vietnam) remained dependent on Chinese inputs, that is, they only served as intermediary producers.

As alternative production sites to supply the West, they suited the strategy named "China plus one (country)". The same applied to certain countries in central Europe, where the stimulus to electric vehicles (EV) had turned China into the largest supplier of EV auto parts outside the EU.

Considering the competition for investments and opportunities, it was clear how countries played both sides, accepting Chinese know-how in the fight for a greater participation in international trade.

**Any reliable numbers?**

Chinese numbers were often seen with a certain degree skepticism, as local statistics were made up to serve Beijing's political interests. In this sense, it is worth highlighting findings from the Federal Reserve (Fed).

Taking into account that official data such as GDP, inflation, and unemployment are published late and, even so, subject to revisions, nothing better than to rely on other sources, such as social media.

Twitter (more recently, just "X"), for example, had shown its value as a tool to capture, with little time lag, trends and expectations regarding the economy, given the large number of tweets.

**Financial sentiment index**

Using posts related to financial topics as a basis, researchers at the Fed were able to create an index. For each positive post, a point in the index and so on.

Exhaustively tested, it not only moved in the same direction as the spreads (differences in the rates) of private bonds in relation to Treasuries, indicating greater risk aversion, but also followed their own yields (market rates).

Other data were quite revealing: posts about people losing their jobs signaled conditions in the labor market, way before official statistics were known.

Its usefulness for measuring the vital signs of the economy were obvious but, with the efforts for users to pay a fee for X (and receive more publicity in return), there are serious doubts about its credibility in the future.

Regardless of what the numbers indicated, it is a fact that the Chinese population is known for its cautious attitude and, having an important part of wealth in the form of real estate, it was unlikely to spend if prices pointed only downwards.

Taking similar episodes from the past as a reference, these circumstances could be reversed by adopting some concepts of Keynesianism, which preached the increase in public spending when other economic agents are unwilling to.

The time had come for Beijing to think of a "plan B" and call its central bank to reduce interest rates, given the ease of coordinating these activities, a privilege of centralized economies.

As it tried to assimilate the long-term impacts after 3 years fighting the pandemic, a period in which money became more expensive and the rules of global trade had changed, China was waiting and so was the rest of the world.

# CHAPTER 12

## BIGGER BRICS

Geopolitics matters and this became clearer than ever in recent times. World growth by globalization, the predominant movement between the years 1990 and 2010, left the scene, giving room to the construction of a web with different motivations.

Unraveling international relations can be a very useful exercise. It's not hard to understand world affairs (and their economic consequences) when one observes that 60 of the 150 largest countries are U.S. allies.

The way these alliances are forged and laws imposed, in an attempt to achieve a desired goal, is part of the geopolitical game. Between smiles and handshakes, each one "neutralizes" its shortcomings by offering "comparative advantages" in return, defined ultimately by geography, climate and natural resources.

### BRICS' origin

At the beginning of the twenty-first century, there was a lot of excitement around the growth of Brazil, Russia, India, and China ("B", "R", "I" and "C" of the BRICS, respectively), which would even compensate for Europe's weak performance, as it focused on the implementation of the euro.

The idea of a specific forum to represent them became reality, with the group's first major event being held in 2009, before South Africa (the "S" of the BRICS) joined in 2010.

But over the next decade, Brazil, Russia, and South Africa lagged behind, as they grew by just 1 percent a year on average, while India and China had numbers six times higher.

The challenge of accommodating such different countries had always been a relevant issue, taking into account their political systems, economic power and military force.

What about their economies? India's GDP per capita was equivalent to 20% of the GDP per capita of China or Russia. While China manages its exchange rate, others already gave up on the idea.

While Russia and Brazil are oil exporters, the rest is highly dependent on imports.

**New format**

The year of 2023 represented the 15th meeting of the group, already transformed by recent geopolitical disruptions. On the agenda, the accession of countries that, in other circumstances, would not even be considered (Argentina, Egypt, Ethiopia, Iran, Saudi Arabia, and United Arab Emirates).

One could even argue what it would defend in its most comprehensive version, given that there was no formal criteria for entering. A common currency and the creation of a new central bank, on the models of the European Central Bank seemed all the most optimistic, given the required sacrifices.

Truth is, until recently, the BRICS served as a forum to expose discontent with the global order, based on the IMF, the World Bank, and the United Nations and its restricted Security Council (although Russia and China are permanent members), in an arrangement that concentrated too much power.

A lot has changed since then. If in the early 2000s the group represented 8% of global GDP, today numbers are around 26%. By way of comparison, during that same period, the G7 was reduced from 65% to 43%.

This meant that even BRICS' laggards stood out on their respective continents, which gave them a certain influence with their neighbors, all to strategic for China, which accounted for 70% of everything the group produced.

## New money

There was no shortage of money to promote such ambitious plans. BRICS has its own versions of the IMF and the World Bank, mentioned before. In the first, it would lend, provided that the other IMF had also done so.

The New Development Bank (NDB), on its part, granted credit to countries that were not BRICS members. Still, the loans were in U.S. dollars or euros, undermining any efforts to lessen the dependency on these currencies.

Everything indicated just a desire to switch sides at the negotiating table. The original five members held 55% of the voting power in the bank. The remaining six, who would be members by 2024, would chip in, with little room to decide what to do with the money.

## Symbolism

All in all, any global order that predominates going forward will not come out of nowhere. It is the result of years of foreign policy work. In the same way, it does not maintain itself by inertia, requiring money and continuous efforts.

Getting the formula right is not one of the easiest

tasks. The power to call the shots (geopolitical influence) depends essentially on economic strength. Maintaining this "status" over time can be a problem when taking into account the cyclical nature of the economy.

The accession of new members was more symbolic than practical, as China had bigger issues at home.

On the external front, its major project (*Belt and Road Initiative*) ran into some limitations, such as the veto by local populations, fearful of environmental impacts, the political cost of employing Chinese workers only, and the fact that China did not feel obliged to join other international creditors in foreign debt renegotiations.

As for the others, it was still unknown what advantages they could obtain, whether in terms of new investments (access to new technologies) or in the form of new financing (money in better conditions, given the high interest rates in the world).

Regardless of individual efforts, the truth is that economic development is accompanied by reforms, which implies leaving behind old ways and making choices, by the leader itself (in the case of monarchies and authoritarian regimes) or by society (in the case of democracies).

With so many interests at stake, choosing a more suitable name for the group would be a good head start.

# CHAPTER 13

## THE NEUTRAL INTEREST RATE

Do central bankers meet just out of formality?

The Federal Reserve proved the opposite. Determined in its fight against inflation, for all the reasons mentioned in Chapter 9, it indicated the possibility of yet another interest rate increase in 2023, emphasizing the restrictive scenario ahead.

The result? A fire sale of assets around the world. Why did that happen? Because everything that is traded in financial markets need to take into account certain peculiarities.

**The debt burden**

US debt continued to rise. Every month, a huge amount of bonds were put up for sale, effectively rolling over debt at higher rates, in an environment with fewer buyers from Asia and the Middle East.

If in the past the first group purchased Treasuries to avoid speculative attacks and the second to invest the revenues from high oil prices, nowadays both had other concerns.

The fact that the Fed also stopped repurchasing bonds as they matured was also an element influencing rates upwards, raising real interest rates, that is, those above inflation.

**Market rates**

At the beginning of 2022, the so-called "quantitative tightening" came into force. It was the opposite of quantitative easing, a mechanism by which the monetary authority reduced long-term interest rates by buying bonds of various maturities.

As a result, the government stopped financing itself at lower costs, by using central bank reserves, to return to bond auctions, at higher market rates.

Considering that Uncle Sam owed the equivalent of 95% of everything the US generated in terms of GDP, investors were prone to demand more in terms of returns. Until the start of the pandemic, the percentage was closer to 80%, showing how much things had changed.

**The unknown neutral rate**

Another argument for the higher for longer monetary policy was the increase in the so-called "neutral rate", which in theory neither stimulates nor discourages the economy.

This neutral interest rate does not change as inflation changes, as it is more affected by structural factors, such as public debt levels, mentioned before, and demographic issues, with effects only perceived in the long-term.

Understanding its dynamics in the economic was the tricky part, given that it is not an observable or even easily measurable variable.

Until the 2008 crisis, it was believed that the neutral rate floated around 4.00% and 4.50% and, once inflation of 2.00% was taken into account, its value would be between 2.00% and 2.50%.

The following decade, however, was one of low inflation and low interest rates, elements that caused the neutral rate to fall to 2.50% (or 0.50% real neutral rate).

As some Fed officials had pointed out, its trend was reversing, returning to higher levels.

What that showed was that a lot could go wrong before interest rates were lowered, benefiting all sorts of asset classes. In the meantime, many held their positions in cash, fearing another increase in yields, which would initiate another mass sale of assets.

Loses were also expected in stock markets, albeit some successful IPOs for chipmakers and artificial intelligence firms (apparently the only game in town).

By and large, there wasn't the slightest motivation in addressing, by some coordinated mechanism, the global imbalances caused by higher interest rates in the US. Currency manipulations, Reagan style, were definitely out as countries pursued other goals.

Cuts in oil production still threatened inflation (prices were back to around US$ 90 per barrel) while China was reluctant to abandon its managed exchange rate system as a way to boost exports and stimulate its economy, so dependent on the real estate sector.

The neutral rate, whatever it might be, could only go higher.

# CHAPTER 14

## WAR IN THE MIDDLE EAST

Oil, throughout history, has always been directly related to economic growth.

Used to build reserves, diversify the economy, exert influence and even attract soccer players, its price is the best indicator of geopolitical risk and, for the Middle East, this could not be different.

With the Hamas attack on October 7th, energy commodity markets opened the following Monday quite jittery. Not because Israel or the Gaza Strip are major oil producers, but because of the fear of a conflict spreading across the region. After all, the first oil shock of the 1970s occurred exactly 50 years ago.

**Embargo**

In 1973, Egypt and Syria coordinated a surprise attack on Israel, which was then celebrating the most important date of the Jewish calendar, Yom Kippur. At that time, the US decided to support Israel.

In the 70's, the world economy was highly dependent on oil, with the Americans barely producing enough to meet its demand (83% of its imports came from the region). The Arab countries, in retaliation, imposed an embargo.

In a period of one year, oil prices rose by more than 300%,

with negative impacts across the world. For the US, the embargo took place when the country was already facing an inflationary scenario, similar to what had happened most recently, which worsened the problem and created a recession.

The revival of the embargo strategy was definitely out of question in this crisis, especially because today the US produces oil more than it consumes, in a world where energy is used more efficiently.

Due to this logic, Americans no longer saw the need to police the Middle East. With the disastrous exit from Afghanistan, they learned that it is always very easy to get into a war, but rather hard to get out of it.

Thus, they were convinced that the best alternative was one where peace is in everyone's interest.

**Abraham Accords**

In recent years, both the United Arab Emirates and Bahrain signed agreements with Israel. Called the "Abraham Accords", they are not just about maintaining peace. Among its objectives, the promotion of regional trade.

Their choice was not by chance. The Gulf countries (Saudi Arabia, Qatar, Bahrain, Kuwait and Oman) represent 60% of the Middle East's GDP and add up to US$3 trillion in reserves deposited with their sovereign wealth funds.

Saudi Arabia, considered the "crown jewel", was in the process of signing its agreement with Israel but, after the attack, froze negotiations. It is no secret that the Saudis defend the Palestinian cause, historically not recognizing the State of Israel.

**The Palestinian cause**

At the beginning of the last century, world power was in the hands of the British Empire. In 1917, the British foreign secretary wrote a short letter in favor of the creation of a State for the Jewish people in Palestine.

After the First World War, Great Britain received the mandate from the League of Nations to rule the Arab country. That's when the Palestinian resistance movement began, culminating in the 1936 revolt.

As a result, the English change their plans, creating resistance among the Jews.

In 1947, the United Nations (UN) splits Palestine, against the will of the Arabs. With the departure of the last English soldiers from the territory the following year, the Jews create the State of Israel. Neighboring Arab countries decide to invade.

With the 1949 armistice, the territory is again divided, between Israel and some of its neighbors. Egypt got hold of the Gaza Strip while Jordan was responsible for the West Bank. Seven hundred thousand Palestinians fled, in what became known as "nakba" (catastrophe, in Arabic).

In the 1967 war, the West Bank is occupied by Israel and, since then, history is punctuated by wars, attacks, revolts, and many diplomatic negotiations, but no Palestinian state.

## The fate of Gaza

Given this explosive past, the war still being fought in Ukraine, high inflation, and low global growth prospects, many feared the repetition of this same destructive pattern.

Looking at the geopolitical complexities, the fate of the Gaza Strip could bring in new developments, which explained the US Secretary of State's tour in the Middle East. Even before the Hamas attack, there were divisions inside Israel, something unthinkable of in its 75 years of existence.

On the military issue, there was the possibility of a two-border war, with Lebanon being on the north, where Hezbollah is positioned. This is exactly what happened in 2006, in another Israeli ground operation in Gaza.

At the time, the militia financed by Iran and who is part of the Lebanese government, surprised the Israeli military forces with its level of sophistication, including in terms of military infrastructure. Today, it looks more like an army, forged by its participation in the wars in Yemen, Syria and Iraq.

Hezbollah, on the other hand, assessed the economic costs of dragging a country shaken by a serious banking crisis in 2019 and the blow up of its Beirut port one year later.

A less bloody alternative was to negotiate with Egypt, affected by the high cost of importing agricultural commodities, such as wheat, since the start of the war in Ukraine and who could have its external debt relieved.

Precedents for such a measure existed. In 1991, the US and other international creditors forgave 25% of Egyptian foreign debt in exchange for military support in the Iraq war.

With the International Monetary Fund (IMF) refusing to release new tranches of a recently signed loan, due to a situation similar to that of Argentina (the central bank issues money to finance government spending), it was believed that Egypt could be willing to talk and, eventually, take in the refugees.

But nowadays, more than half of Egypt's external debt is in the hands of the Arabs (United Arab Emirates, Qatar and Saudi Arabia), who were now observing the disastrous result of the current Israeli government's policy towards the Palestinians.

With so many variables at play, all eyes turned to oil prices, once again.

# CHAPTER 15

## THE ECONOMICS OF WAR

The second stage of the war in Gaza promised to be a long one.

Destroying Hamas' infrastructure, made up of a labyrinth of underground tunnels, and removing the group from power had many risks, considering the densely populated urban area and the hostage issue, things which would, among other things, reinforce the pressure for a humanitarian ceasefire, as it had occurred at a recent United Nations General Assembly.

Between attacks and brief periods of truce, until the leadership vacuum was resolved and an exit plan established, the focus remained on mobilization for war, imposing significant economic costs.

**War economy**

A characteristic of economies at war is the production for war purposes, although this process is not automatic. Chaos takes over in the beginning, as economic agents digest the future fall in GDP, resulting from those who decide to leave, are called to fight, or even stay to care of the wounded.

For no other reason, the first blow is felt in the country's own currency.  Consumer goods industries are then reorganized, with activities coordinated by the military.

Businesses run on the "war intelligence" they obtain, making use of the few resources available (energy, water, fuel, and communication networks are the targets usually attacked by the enemy).

Even in the least affected regions, long lines and empty shelves. After all, troops need to be fed and transported. In the war effort, even exports are sacrificed.

## The economy in Israel

In 2021, Tel Aviv ranked first in the list of the world's most expensive cities, displacing Paris.

The position in the ranking was due to the appreciation of the Israeli currency, a consequence of the fast return to normality after the pandemic, in addition to the significant weight of its technology ecosystem.

Two years later and with a war looming, the shekel fell to levels not seen in at least ten years, prompting Israel's central bank to sell $30 billion of its reserves. In the meantime, insuring against government default became prohibitive.

Expectations were of increased public spending, in a scenario where there would be no consumers to stimulate the economy and much less tourists.

## Debt burden

In this sense, some of the measures implemented during the pandemic could be used again, such as business support programs, tax deferrals, in addition to aid for those displaced to other regions.

Despite a healthy debt-to-GDP ratio of only 60 percent, the bill would bloat as every war has a start date but no end date.

Calling up more than 360,000 reservists, or about 8

percent of the workforce, also meant mobilizing highly productive people.    Since the beginning of October, 70% of the country's most innovative companies found difficulty functioning, which meant fewer opportunities when people returned home.

At the end of the day, no industry was immune.  Even for low-skilled jobs, economic activity was hampered as insecurity prevented Palestinians, mainly from the West Bank, from entering Israel to show up for work.

This was the pattern of previous "intifadas" (revolts), indicating a yearly GDP 25% lower than anticipated.

**The economic war**

In 1994, the UN coordinated an agreement where Israel, the Gaza Strip and the West Bank would share a common market.   Palestinians were allowed to work in Israel or Israeli settlements, a decision that would boost their respective economies.

However, executing the integration plan was more difficult, mainly because of such big disparities between them.   Currently, some 25% of Palestinians in the West Bank got jobs "on the other side," with the figure being infinitely lower for Gaza, which saw its economy shrink.

There, the economic war had been going on for a long time. Between 2007, when Hamas seized power, and 2022, its population impoverished by 2.5% each year.   The wars fought in this period (2008, 2014, and 2021) took away, individually, the equivalent of an annual GDP.

**The aid economy**

Highly dependent on some form of aid, more than half of the adult population in the enclave was already living below the poverty line two years before, according to estimates by the International Monetary Fund (IMF).

The money that circulated in its economy came from elsewhere. In addition to the Palestinian Authority (PA) and some Gulf countries, schools and hospitals were maintained by the UN and other international bodies.

The energy consumed in Gaza and supplied by Israel was paid by the Palestinian Authority as Israel deducted a part of the import taxes it collects on its behalf in the West Bank, where the PA has administrative autonomy.

Hamas, for its part, maintained its governing structure by levying taxes on everything it imported from Egypt and the West Bank, as well as taxing income.

The only viable economic activity in Gaza was restricted to the construction sector, for obvious reasons.

**The end of the "peace dividend"**

With the end of the Cold War and the fall of the Soviet Union in the early 1990s, the world benefited from the so-called "peace dividend."

Resources previously spent on the military front geared economic growth, in the form of infrastructure and public services. Governments were given the option of reducing public debt or granting tax incentives.

Three decades later, the arms race returned, inflating ammunition prices and swelling defense budgets, now jockeying for space with climate goals and the pension costs of an aging global population.

In 2022, when Ukraine was invaded, the country issued bonds to raise money for the war effort. With interest rates much higher the following year and two wars going on simultaneously, who would risk buying them?

# CHAPTER 16

## ARGENTINA AND THE DOLLAR

Javier Milei won the presidential elections on the promise of adopting the US dollar as the main currency in Argentina.

Before him, a 3-digit inflation and barely any international reserves. The local currency was worth half its value at the beginning of 2023.

Within the International Monetary Fund (IMF), everyone talked about it. In the last 65 years, the country was bailed out 22 times. In 2018, it received the largest loan ever granted by the institution (US$ 57 billion).

With its swollen public sector (equivalent to 38% of GDP) and the social benefits granted by previous governments, it made ends meet borrowing from China, and in its own currency, the yuan.

With such an economic disorder, would dollarization "reset" things? How would that work exactly?

**Dollarization**

Simply put, it is a process where the local currency is replaced by the US dollar. The country gives up its monetary policy, which is then dictated by the Federal Reserve (Fed), the US central bank.

Among its advantages, predictability and the gradual way

by which interest rates are adjusted. Due to this, lower asset volatility, regardless of local circumstances.

Additionally, the inconvenience and costs of currency conversions become a thing of the past, given that in problematic economies, the population tries to maintain some purchasing power by saving US dollars and, until the explosion of FTX, cryptocurrencies.

As a disadvantage, the impossibility of printing more money. Nowadays, it is a fact that governments are forced into more spending and, in Latin America, this could not be different.

Theoretically, by restricting spending, governments adjust their budgets and privatize, addressing out-of-control inflation, as the public sector is streamlined and inefficient companies fixed for good.

In practical terms, abandoning the local currency can lead to two different paths. The adoption of dollarization itself or the implementation of a "currency board", occasion on which the money in circulation is backed by dollar reserves at the central bank, thus preventing the printing of more money.

The first option is the most credible, but it imposes greater sacrifices and is difficult to reverse, as the monetary authority uses its reserves to purchase the local currency. In the second one, however, reserves are maintained, earning interest.

Looking back at history, would dollarization suit Argentina? How did other countries fare in that matter?

**Ecuador**

Ecuador went through this process 23 years ago.

Facing a political crisis and a huge currency devaluation, resulting from the drop in its economic activity followed by a default (non-payment) on its renegotiated external debt (Brady Bonds), the country decided to dollarize in early 2000.

Just like Argentina in 2023, the local economy was heading towards hyperinflation and, under these circumstances, easing monetary policy as a form of stimulus is not an alternative.

Ecuador followed the most difficult path and stability came quickly, even though other distortions remained. The fiscal deficit (public spending greater than what the government collects in the form of taxes) continued, which led to the use of creative accounting.

In 2019, the country was forced to knock on the IMF's door.

**El Salvador**

Discussions about the adoption of bitcoin aside, El Salvador observed Ecuador's implementation mistakes and tried its own version, in a more organized way. Its currency was pegged to the dollar since 1994, which helped to replace it.

Giving up the local currency made sense. Approximately 67% of what was exported at the time was shipped to the US, with the country still receiving around US$2 billion in the form of remittances, sent by immigrants to their families.

Its political system was a pro-market one, which means that the government had a reduced role in the economy. With this, it was able to obtain an advantage that is normally granted at a later stage of dollarization: cheaper credit, which favors economic growth.

Even so, not everything was solved there. First, because neighboring countries, with devalued currencies, were more competitive. Second, because the country was hit by earthquakes, causing public debt (reconstruction spending) to grow to 3.7% of GDP, impacting financing costs.

As it is clear, dollarization goes hand in hand with reforms, including in the banking sector, which stops hiding its inefficiencies, whether internal or regulatory, under the economic chaos.

Reverting Argentina's fortunes came down to gaining the political strength to approve extremely unpopular measures, something that is yet to be seen under Milei's government.

Besides, the Federal Reserve has commitments with the US government and the US banking system, but has no obligations whatsoever with the Argentine government or its local banks.

If anyone cared to draw a parallel with the crisis faced by some US banks at the beginning of the year (chapter 2), it would be easy to realize that the impacts would be catastrophic if something went wrong.

Without an established mechanism to provide liquidity and avoid contagion in the Argentine financial system, there would basically be a collective default by the government, banks, companies, and people.

To avoid collapse, the country would have to turn again to the same IMF, like Ecuador, but in an infinitely worse situation. The organization already holds approximately a third of all the country's foreign debt and continues to lend.

Last but not least, it is worth noting that the US economy, unlike Argentina, was performing well, which meant that interest rates applicable to the dollar would remain high for a long time. Given the lack of synch between the two countries, what were the real benefits of a strong dollar for Argentinians?

For all the reasons in the world, other people's currency can bring more problems than solutions.

# CHAPTER 17

## DUBAI AND COP28

A big climate event hosted by a petrostate. The COP held at the UAE had a record number of participants and much of the luxury Dubai is known for.

Government representatives and non-profit climate organizations are usually the kind of people that show up. At COP28 however, oil company bosses did participate.

Goals set by the Paris Agreement were nowhere near, as delegates acknowledged that, no matter the intention, climate policies not necessarily reach the desired effect, due basically to the multitude of interests involved.

Orchestrated by a body inside the United Nations, the COP aims specifically to center stage the topic and bring awareness on a global problem with long-term disastrous consequences, something the political calendar in democracies fails to accommodate, as it imposes costs on today's voters.

Luckily, the $28^{th}$ event counted with a supportive agreement by the heavyweights of China and the US in the methane discussions. Oil and gas companies joined through their pledges to do more, not least to be able to sell to the EU, where climate regulation is stricter.

Party distractions aside, one important message aired in the many negotiation rooms is that there is no magic when it comes to solutions to fight climate change. Clean energy technologies, including nuclear power, require lots of funding.

Will this money come from the sale of more oil and gas by OPEC member states like the UAE?

Additionally, rich countries were reluctant to let the loss and damage fund turn into a blank check they have to provide to poorer countries suffering the impacts of climate change.

With governments grappling with new international requirements and expensive money, the only way to deal with climate change is to provide the right incentives so that the private sector can fill the gap and thrive, without baking the planet.

# CHAPTER 18


## THE FUTURE


The year of 2024 will feature an unprecedented number: 4.2 billion, roughly more than half of the world's population, will go to the polls, with the election in the US being the most prominent.

Even before the race officially began, Donald Trump had a 33% chance of winning, with his proposals to reduce taxes for the Americans while fighting with the rest of the world, through additional tariffs.

Politics aside, his chances could change depending on his views about the US debt, continuously growing, or the climate agenda, after so many subsidies for renewable sources. Needless to say, both are issues with global impacts.

There is clearly the need for new world order, as two wars in just two years show. Today, the G7 economies represent less than half of the world's GDP. Countries admittedly are acting together or alone, regardless of any effort by the US to dictate the rules, unlike the 90s, when globalization was the main moving force.

In other words, they are no longer attracted by common goals such as a market economy and integrated international trade, an impractical arrangement considering sanctions of all kinds. Whoever offers more in terms of financial benefits will win whatever game is played, even if transactions are conducted in another currency, such as the yuan.

China will no doubt try to fill this global leadership vacuum, whether financing infrastructure projects, as it has done for quite a while, whether lending reserves, as the case of Argentina shows. How much it will achieve in terms of growth in the process is another matter.

It will gain new partners by exploring the idea of continuity, of a government that fulfills what it sets out to do, without the political risks of power changing hands at each election. In this other war ("cold war"), alliances also matter.

Demand for oil and gas will continue high as the planet heats up, with all the geopolitical factors associated with energy commodities, while the world creates the necessary infrastructure for the energy transition.

Thus, it will not be a case of one (fossil) or the other (renewable), but of one and (also) the other, creating the same perverse and cyclical dynamic for metals, where higher prices favor the opening of new mines which, when completed, face an already bloated market.

The truth is that the future will require resources for a little bit of everything: competitiveness in the extraction of fossil fuels and metals, in addition to economic growth, which will be increasingly dependent on essentially intermittent energy sources.

How to fund all this is the big question, and not just for 2024. If governments need to spend more, how compatible are high interest rates and high public debt? If rates are to remain high for longer, what is the deadline for inflation to be declared over?

As mentioned before, elections will be held in many places next year. Usually, it is a time when anything can happen, except less government spending.

In other words, economies that were already facing difficulties in external financing since the pandemic, either because they owe money to the IMF or because they were bailed out by China, may not find any doors open.

The result could be more popular uprisings, fueling the geopolitical chaos.

Will AI, the great productivity promise of our times help economies grow out of this mess or will it just make things worse?

# Nohad T. Harati

has a degree in business administration in addition to both an MBA in finances and an LLM in financial market law from a prestigious Brazilian educational institution (Insper).

She started her career at a local commodities broker, becoming a private banking investment analyst for a Swiss financial institution a few years later.

She also participated as an alternate board member at Companhia Energética de Minas Gerais (CEMIG), a Brazilian energy distribution company.

Currently, she manages a proprietary portfolio, runs a family office and is a regular columnist for the Brazilian investment startup Mais Retorno (https://maisretorno.com/portal/autor/nohadharati) in addition to publishing articles in her own personal pages:

LinkedIn: https://www.linkedin.com/in/nohadharati/
Quora (English): https://www.quora.com/profile/Nohad-Harati
Quora (Portuguese): https://pt.quora.com/profile/Nohad-Harati